JULIE ED...

1313 EG...

MOUNT VERNON 98274

Stories of
JESUS

Text by Juliet David
Illustrations by Elina Ellis
Copyright © 2019 ZipAddress Limited

Published by
Lion Hudson Limited
Wilkinson House, Jordan Hill Business Park,
Banbury Road, Oxford OX2 8DR, England
www.lionhudson.com

ISBN 978 1 78128 357 8

First edition 2019

A catalogue record for this book is available from the British Library

Printed and bound in China, August 2019, LH54

Stories of
JESUS

BY JULIET DAVID
ILLUSTRATED BY ELINA ELLIS

CANDLE
BOOKS

Lost in Jerusalem

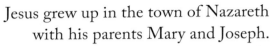

Jesus grew up in the town of Nazareth with his parents Mary and Joseph. Every year the Jewish people went to Jerusalem for a great festival.

When Jesus was twelve, Mary said, "This year you can come with us."

During the festival, they visited the Temple, where Jesus met teachers and priests.

Soon it was all over and they started the long walk back home to Nazareth.

That night Joseph and Mary suddenly realized they hadn't seen Jesus all day.

They walked all the way back to Jerusalem to look for him.

Finally they found Jesus. He was back in the Temple!
Jesus had stayed there for days, talking to the teachers and priests.
"Didn't you guess I'd be here?" Jesus asked Mary.
"I came to my Father's house, to learn what I need to know."

John baptizes Jesus

John was Jesus' cousin. He lived in the desert.

   Some people asked John, "Are you the one God is sending to save us?"

   "Someone greater than me is coming," he told them.

   One day Jesus came to John beside the River Jordan.

   "Please baptize me!" Jesus said to John.

10

"But I should be baptized by *you*," said John.
"There's no way I should baptize you!"
   "But it's what God wants!" Jesus replied.
   So John agreed. He dipped Jesus in the River Jordan.
   When Jesus came out of the water, a dove appeared.
   And a voice said, "This is my Son. I'm very pleased with him."

11

Jesus chooses a team

One day Jesus was standing beside Lake Galilee.

Lots of people crowded around, listening to his wonderful stories.

Jesus climbed into one of the boats on the beach. It belonged to Simon Peter.

"Push the boat out a bit," said Jesus.

Then he talked to the people from the boat.

When he had finished, Jesus said to Simon Peter, "Push out into deeper water and let down your nets. You can catch plenty of fish."

"We've fished all night and not caught a thing," said Simon Peter. "But if you say so, I'll let down the nets again."

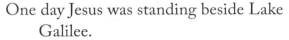

12

This time their nets were so full they began to tear.

Simon Peter, his brother Andrew, and their friends, James and John, were amazed to see so many fish.

Jesus told them, "Come, follow me! From now on, you'll be fishing for people!"

They all followed Jesus.

They were the first of Jesus' special friends, the disciples.

More special friends

People didn't like tax collectors.

They cheated people and took too much money.

One day Jesus saw a tax collector called Matthew working at his desk.

"Follow me!" he called.

At once Matthew got up, left his job, and followed Jesus. He became one of Jesus' special friends.

Jesus called some more men: Philip, Bartholomew, Thomas the twin, another James, Thaddaeus, Simon, and Judas Iscariot.

There were twelve altogether.

They all became Jesus' special friends, the disciples.

Jesus goes to a party

One day a man invited Jesus to his wedding party.

Jesus' mother, Mary, was there too, and Jesus' special friends.

Everyone was eating and drinking. It wasn't long before they'd finished all the wine. Now what could they drink?

"Fill those six stone jars with water!" said Jesus.
The men did as Jesus told them.
Immediately the water changed into wine.
"This is the best wine we've ever tasted!" people said.
Jesus made sure that wedding party went really well!

A blind man sees

One day Jesus was visiting a village near Jerusalem.
Some friends brought a blind man to him.
"Please help our blind friend to see!" they begged Jesus.
Jesus took the man's hand and led him out of the village.

Jesus placed his hands over the blind man's eyes.
His eyes opened. Now the blind man could see clearly.
Jesus helped this blind man see!

The man who thanked

As Jesus was walking along the road, he met ten men.
They didn't come close, because they all had a skin disease called leprosy.
   The men called out to Jesus, "Please help us!"
   "You are healed," Jesus told them, and he sent them on their way.
   Sure enough, as the men walked home, the disease vanished.
   One man returned to thank Jesus for healing him.
   "Where are the other nine?" asked Jesus.
"Only this man – a foreigner – came back to thank God."

21

Jesus gives life to a girl

A man called Jairus came to Jesus. He was very worried.
"My little girl is terribly ill," he said. "Please help me!"
Jesus hurried home with Jairus.

But by the time they arrived, Jairus' daughter had died.

Jesus took her hand. "Little girl, wake up!" he said.
At once she opened her eyes.
"Give her something to eat!" Jesus said to her mother.
Jesus helped the little girl come back to life.

A man through the roof

Another time some friends carried a sick man to Jesus.

The house where Jesus was teaching was so full that they had to climb on the roof and tear a hole in it to get near to Jesus.

The friends lowered the sick man carefully down.
Jesus saw the man couldn't walk,
yet he said, "Stand up!"
At once the sick man
stood up.
Everyone watching
was astonished.
Jesus helped this
disabled man to
walk.

A very hungry crowd

One time Jesus went into the country.

Lots of people followed him, so Jesus told them stories all day.

By the time evening came, everyone felt hungry.

But they had almost nothing to eat!

One boy had brought with him just five loaves and two fish.

He gave them all to Jesus.

Jesus broke up the bread and the fish.

Then his friends gave out the food.

There was enough for everyone!

Even after they had all eaten, there were twelve baskets of leftovers.

Jesus fed this hungry crowd.

It was a wonderful miracle!

Jesus walks on the lake

Later that day, Jesus told his friends to sail across the lake.

"I will follow later," he said.

The disciples got into their boat and set sail.

It grew dark, and when they were halfway across the lake a strong wind came up.

The men rowed hard to prevent the boat sinking.

Then they saw something very frightening.

They thought it was a ghost!

But it was Jesus, walking to them on the water.

"Don't be afraid!" he called out to them.

He got into the boat – and the wind calmed down immediately.

29

The lost son

Jesus told this great story.

There was once a farmer who had two sons.

The younger son left home, taking his share of his father's money.

The boy went to a distant country.
He had lots of money, so he had lots of friends – and lots of parties.
When his money ran out, the son's friends disappeared too.

So he found a job looking after pigs.
He was so hungry that he even ate the pigs' food!

One day the boy thought, "I'd be better off as a servant in my father's house than feeding these pigs."

So he set off back home. It was a very long walk. But his father was waiting to welcome him.

His father gave a great party.

"Rejoice!" he said. "My son, who was lost, is found!"

Jesus added, "God also welcomes people who are lost."

The stranger who helped

Another day Jesus told this story.

A man was walking from Jerusalem to Jericho,
when all of a sudden robbers attacked him.

They stole everything he had, and left him lying on the road.

Later, a priest came along. He should have helped.

He saw the injured man, but passed quickly by.

Then a man who worked at the temple came along.
He noticed the man in the road. But he walked straight past too.

Finally, a stranger came down the road. When he saw the injured man,
he jumped down from his donkey, and cleaned the man's wounds.
Then he took the poor man to an inn to be looked after.

"Which of these men was a true friend?" Jesus asked.

"The stranger," someone said.

"Yes!" said Jesus. "Now go and treat everyone you meet the same way."

The missing sheep

Jesus told this story too.

A shepherd once had one hundred sheep.

One night he lost one of these sheep, so he set off to look for it.

He was out most of the night searching.

At last the shepherd found his missing sheep.

He picked it up gently and carried it home.

The shepherd called his friends together.

"Be happy!" he said. "I've found my lost sheep."

"God is like the good shepherd," said Jesus.

"He's glad when anyone comes to him."

34

Love like a little child!

Lots of people wanted to see Jesus.
When Jesus saw how sad and ill some were,
he wanted to help them.
One day some mothers brought their
children to Jesus.
His disciples started sending
them away.
"Jesus is tired," they
said. "Don't pester
him now with your
children!"
But Jesus heard
what they were
saying.
"Let the little children
come to me!" he said.
"Don't stop them!
You must love God like a little child
if you want to enter heaven."

When the wind blew

Another time Jesus was sailing across the lake with his friends.

He was so tired that he fell asleep.

All of a sudden a great storm blew.

The disciples were very frightened.

They knew how dangerous it could be on the lake.

"Jesus, wake up!" they shouted.

"We're all going to drown."

Jesus stood up.

"Storm – be quiet!" he shouted.

"Wind – stop blowing!"

Suddenly, everything was calm.

Jesus helped his friends when they were very scared.

Jesus and the captain

One day an army captain came to Jesus.

"My servant is very ill," he said.

"Then I'll come and help him," said Jesus.

"Just say the word – and my servant will be well," said the captain.

Jesus was astonished.

"I've never met *anyone* who trusted me so much!" he said.

"Go home!" Jesus told the captain.

"What you have asked for will happen."

Sure enough, when the captain arrived home,
he found his servant was already well again.

Jesus had healed the captain's servant.

A tiny man meets Jesus

In the town of Jericho lived a man called Zacchaeus. He collected tax money.

But Zacchaeus was a bad man. He took more money than he should. People hated him!

Zacchaeus heard that Jesus was visiting Jericho.

Zacchaeus was very short, so he climbed a tree to make sure he had a good view.

But then Zacchaeus got a real shock! Jesus stopped under his tree.

"Come down, Zacchaeus!" Jesus called up to him. "I want to have dinner at your house."

And he did! Over their meal, Jesus talked about the bad things Zacchaeus was doing.

Now Zacchaeus wanted to change.

"I'm going to give half my money to the poor," he told Jesus.

41

The fish that paid

One day Peter, one of Jesus' disciples, said,
"It's time to pay our tax money!"

Jesus had no money. Nor did Peter.

But Jesus knew just what to do.

"Go to the lake and catch a fish!" Jesus told Peter.
"You'll find a coin in the fish's mouth. Use that to pay our tax."

Peter quickly caught a fish.

He opened its mouth – and, sure enough, there was a silver coin!

Peter took it to pay the tax man.

Jesus had done another of his miracles.

Other titles in the series